Baby and Beyond

Progression in Play for Babies and Children

First Role Play

Baby and Beyond - Role Play

ISBN 1 906029 02 4 • 978 1 906029 02 9

© Featherstone Education Ltd, 2007

Text © Sally Featherstone and Liz Williams, 2007; Illustrations © Martha Hardy, 2007; Series Editor, Sally Featherstone

First published in the UK, August 2007

'Baby and Beyond' is a trade mark of Featherstone Education Ltd

Published in the United Kingdom by

Featherstone Education Ltd, 44 - 46 High Street, Husbands Bosworth, Leicestershire, LE17 6LP

Printed in the UK on paper produced in the European Union from managed, sustainable forests

Contents

Baby and Beyond

A series of books for practitioners working with children from birth to five and beyond

This book gives ideas for introducing and extending role play activities and experiences for babies and young children. Each page spread contains a range of experiences and a selection of ideas for each of the developmental stages of the Early Years Foundation Stage (EYFS). We have retained the descriptive names of the four earlier developmental stages from Birth to Three Matters, while adjusting the age ranges to cover the whole EYFS:

Birth - 11 months	8 - 20 months	16 - 26 months	22 - 40 months	40 - 60+ months
Heads up Lookers and Communicators	Sitters, Standers and Explorers	Movers, Shakers and Players	Walkers, Talkers and Pretenders	Moving on

Role play is natural to all children. It is the way they make sense of the experiences they have and the world they inhabit. Very young children are still exploring things at close range and may do this through schemas or repeated activities, and these may include collecting things in containers, putting items of clothing on and taking them off, and copying the actions of older children and adults.

From the time when they first recognise themselves as separate beings, children will begin to 'try on' the clothing, actions, speech and mannerisms of the important people in their lives. This may involve them in brushing their hair with a toothbrush because they recognise the shape of the brush, wearing items of adult clothing or 'feeding' a doll or teddy. Creative thinking, asking questions, solving problems and making links in learning are all elements in the process of playing in role, and often children will get involved in this play with their whole bodies. However, the use of puppets, dolls, soft toys and small world characters will also be used by children to explore their feelings and the world around them, so practitioners should make sure all these forms of play are available to children. Sometimes a child will find it easier to express how they feel or what they are thinking by using a soft toy, puppet or small world character. We have all experienced how a frustrated, confused or unhappy child may express their anger or sadness by telling off a teddy or using a model superhero to demolish a play situation.

As a practitioner you will already know how important role play is to young children, and this book is intended to help you to extend your support for children's creative play. The book is laid out in progressions across the Early Years Foundation Stage, each covering one aspect of role play at five different developmental stages. We have tried to give you ideas which build on your own creativity and don't involve you in large purchases or time consuming preparation. For most children, the permission to be creative, the time to develop their play, and the provision of a range of flexible resources is all they need as they set off on their creative explorations. Of course, younger children may need more of your time and help, and older children need to see this play as important to you, so you do need to accompany children as they play. This will give you opportunities to observe and learn about them as individuals and groups, and to help them solve problems and develop their learning. This sustained shared thinking, where adults and small groups of children work together as equal partners is a key to high quality provision and is a central element in the Early Years Foundation Stage. Practitioners need to stand back and resist the temptation to dominate the play, and we realise that this is difficult, but if you can support high quality, independent role play for children of all ages in your setting, then you will be offering the children in your care a chance to become creative thinkers, collaborative workers, problem solvers and skilled technicians!

Other books you might find useful: The Little Book of Role Play; The Little book of Prop Boxes for Role Play; The Little Book of Small World Play; The Little Book of Outdoor Play; What If? role play packs; Inside Out; all available from Featherstone Education Ltd. on 01858 881212 or www.featherstone.uk.com

| 0-11 months | 8-20 months | 16 - 26 months | 22 - 40 months | 40 - 60+ months |

| Heads Up, Lookers and Communicators | Sitters, Standers and Explorers | Movers, Shakers and Players | Walkers, Talkers and Pretenders | Moving on |

Inspiring Creativity

Role play is a key way in which young children learn. The practitioner's job is to inspire imaginative and role play by providing flexible resources for children of all ages, and encouraging creative use of these with children, demonstrating and modelling creative thinking and play.

Young babies (0-11 months)

A piece of fabric draped round your shoulders, a pair of sunglasses, a red nose or a funny hat will all grab the attention of babies. Let the baby look at, feel and explore the simple role play resources you are modelling. Use a silly or funny voice, move in a different way, or sing a song as you have a game together. As babies begin to control their hands, they will grab objects you are wearing, so make sure these are both safe and dribble proof!

Heads Up, Lookers and Communicators

Babies (8-20 months)

Offering small squares of different sorts of fabrics, bags and scarves will fascinate babies, even before they are standing and moving around. They will experiment with draping and scrunching fabrics to see how they feel, often stroking their own cheeks and arms to feel them. Sit with them as they explore, draping fabrics round your own shoulders, putting on hats and scarves and trying on gloves and shoes.

Sitters, Standers and Explorers

Young children (16-26 months)

Provide dressing up resources that are a mixture of unstructured materials such as fabrics, boxes and bags; everyday dressing up clothes such as scarves, shoes, socks, gloves and hats for children and adults; and items made for specific uses such as fire helmets, fairy dresses, or themed items from TV or films. Don't put out too much at a time. Change the items frequently and limit them to just a few items at a time. This will stimulate play and reduce the muddle!

Movers, Shakers and Players

Children (22-40 months)

Check the use and contents of role play boxes frequently to make sure they are interesting and have fresh items to inspire new play. Monitor use of the items by both boys and girls, by playing alongside them and showing your own creativity. Talk about new items for the role play boxes at group time, discussing how they might be used and who might use them. Look in 'Pound' shops and charity shops for cheap inspiration and new resources.

Walkers, Talkers and Pretenders

Older children (40-60+ months)

Encourage older children to make their own props, hats, masks and clothes by making suggestions, working with them and offering the sorts of recycled resources they can use to make these. Adding their own props (boxes, hats, masks, containers etc.) expands on the creative experience and increases children's sense of ownership of their play. Help them to make props that link with their current interests or playing out familiar stories, characters and rhymes.

Moving on

Hats and Shoes

Collect as many hats and different shoes as you can. Children love wearing other people's shoes and a hat is all some children need to get into character. Check your setting's Health and Safety guidance on the use of second hand clothing and use your judgement about where these come from! Change these items frequently.

Young babies (0-11 months)

Putting a hat on your head and letting the baby tip it off is an activity all babies love. They will often want to repeat this for longer than you are prepared to do it! Try putting the hat on the baby and tipping it off yourself. Go gently if this is a new experience, and try with different sorts and sizes of hats - caps, bobble hats, sunhats, baby hats - trying them on yourself as well, or holding the baby up to a mirror so they can see themselves and you wearing the hats.

Heads Up, Lookers and Communicators

Babies (8-20 months)

As babies get more independent, they love having a go at putting on shoes and hats themselves, and will often put them on and take them off repeatedly. Just offer them one hat or a pair of easy shoes and see what happens. You may need to model the activity yourself first and then encourage them to have a go. Floor level mirrors make this activity even more interesting for the babies, and you could take some photos of them for a personal photo book or display.

Sitters, Standers and Explorers

Young children (16-26 months)

As children begin to relate to story book and TV characters, they love to wear the hats that identify them - Bob the Builder, Fireman Sam, pirates and other story characters. Often a hat alone will be enough to get a child completely into role. They also love to be grown up, using the hats and particularly the shoes of adults they know. Women's shoes, even those with low heels, sandals, flip flops, boots and training shoes can all be added to simple role play boxes and bags.

Movers, Shakers and Players

Children (22-40 months)

At this stage, children really enter into pretend play, and need a constant supply of hats and shoes to feed their creativity. Often a box or basket of shoes and hats (nothing else) will keep these pretenders busy all day, as they collect or substitute the other items they need for their play. Headbands with ears, feathers or hair can transform a child into another person or animal. You can also use simple woollen hats or caps as bases for fantasy hats.

Walkers, Talkers and Pretenders

Older children (40-60+ months)

If children are used to inventing their own clothing from basic materials such as fabric strips, headbands, hats and shoes, they will enter into the spirit of decorating or adding to garments to create new versions. Offer them card, feathers, sequins, fabrics, fabric pens, badges and other simple additions to make their own hats and decorate shoes, wellington boots, plimsols or slippers. Adding reflective tape to black wellies will transform them into boots for firemen.

Moving on

Scarves and Ribbons

Scarves, ribbons and fabric strips have hundreds of uses in role play. Make sure you have plenty of these long strips to offer for creative and fantasy play. Get scarves from charity shops or ask parents and friends to donate them. Cut strips from stretchy material that doesn't fray, and get ribbon remnants from markets. Make sure babies and younger children are well supervised to avoid tangling and tying round their necks.

Young babies (0-11 months)

Thread bells on ribbon or stretchy fabric and attach to babies' wrists or ankles so they jingle as the baby moves. Use scarves to wrap round arms and legs (don't leave babies alone with long lengths of material - they may get tangled in them). Hang ribbons or strips of material from door frames or baby gyms so they sway in the wind and attract eyes and fingers. Attach ribbon securely to decorate baby chairs and bouncers.

Heads Up, Lookers and Communicators

Babies (8-20 months)

Once babies can grab and pull, put lots of scarves and strips of fabrics in a basket for them to pull out. Help them to wind these round their arms and legs as you play with them (making sure they are not left alone). Hang ribbons and strings to door frames, above changing tables and play spaces, so babies can learn how they move, and feel their textures. Tie feathers and other small objects to the ends for added interest.

Sitters, Standers and Explorers

Young children (16-26 months)

Long strips of fabric are essential elements of good role play, and children will begin to use them for all sorts of purposes as they create their games and stories. 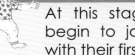 They can be tied to soft toys or wheeled toys as leads, strung between furniture and frames for fences and enclosures, wrapped round parts of their bodies for bandages or decoration or laid on the floor as paths and boundaries.

Movers, Shakers and Players

Children (22-40 months)

At this stage, children may begin to join strips together with their first knots. As you see this need emerging, you may have to help, but don't take over! Children may get interested in making long strings with lengths of ribbon, strips of fabric or string. These may not be for anything, just a joining schema, so watch for this. Other children may use the strips for more wrapping, or tie them to bikes and other wheeled toys.

Walkers, Talkers and Pretenders

Older children (40-60+ months)

Children who have an interest in super-heroes may begin to use fabric strips, stretchy scarves and headbands to make armbands, headbands and belts for superhero play. This is a good creative channel for a very popular sort of activity. Other children may use scarves and ribbons for long hair, for decoration or to make screens and boundaries to their play spaces. Using outdoor equipment such as climbing frames for role play may spark a request to make flags!

Moving on

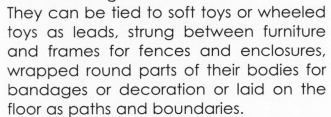

Fabrics to Wear

To support good early role play, it is not necessary to buy ready made sets of clothing from suppliers. This often stereotypes children's play, can be gender specific and limits children's creativity. Fabrics of different sizes, weights, patterns and textures will do more to encourage creative play and only need the addition of a few hats and props.

Young babies (0-11 months)

Explore textures of fabrics with babies, stroking your cheeks with them, feeling them against hand and arms, hanging them up to wave in the breeze, or sitting with them in your lap. Try wrapping some fabric gently round both you and the baby, holding the baby securely on your knee or in your arms, but not restricting their movements. Use fabrics as head coverings and capes together and look at yourselves in a mirror.

Heads Up, Lookers and Communicators

Babies (8-20 months)

Sitting babies will enjoy being offered pieces of fabric in a shallow basket. Keep these small enough for them to handle, but big enough to cover their hand or head (40-50cm is about right). Offer some net curtaining or transparent materials so they can look at the world through a veil or shawl. Sit with the babies and enjoy wearing the fabrics yourself over your head, shoulders or arms. Talk about what you are doing and praise their efforts. Enjoy yourselves!

Sitters, Standers and Explorers

Young children (16-26 months)

As they begin to be more independent and gain a sense of self, low level mirrors are very useful additions. These should show the whole child and reach down to the floor. Just put a basket of pieces of fabric by a mirror and see what happens. If children have not had experience of this sort of play before, sit with them and explore the fabrics, talking about what they are like, and how they move, then try using them to decorate yourselves and each other.

Movers, Shakers and Players

Children (22-40 months)

As children get interested in joining, add some plastic, soft-grip clothes pegs to the basket of fabrics, so children can help each other to dress up. Expand the range of types and sizes of fabric, but don't make the pieces too big or they become unmanageable. You could also add some ribbons and scarves to expand the opportunities for turning yourself into someone else. Both boys and girls love this sort of play and turn themselves into all sorts of people.

Walkers, Talkers and Pretenders

Older children (40-60+ months)

Encourage children to use the pieces of fabric to make more complex creative costumes by offering fabric pens, glitter, lace, buttons, feathers and edging to decorate the pieces of fabric. You could offer squares and rectangles of sheeting (eg by cutting up old bed sheets) so the children can make their own garments, cutting head holes, and sticking or pinning pieces of other fabrics in place before adding sequins and other decorations with glue and paint. These could be used for impromptu plays and stories made up by the children, or for retelling favourite stories.

Moving on

15

Fabrics to Drape and Cover

Bigger pieces of washable fabric are essential for den making and creative play both indoors and outside. These pieces can be draped, laid flat, suspended, joined or wrapped round trees, vehicles, furniture, boxes (or anything else) on grass, paving, the floor, or hung from washing lines, fences or canes.

Young babies (0-11 months)

Cover a floor cushion with a shiny piece of satin or some velvet for a special place for a snuggle. Or drape a big piece of fabric over chairs for a secret hideout for you and a baby. Babies love to lie on different textures of fabrics, so collect fleece, fur fabric, silks, soft wools and shiny sparkly fabrics. Avoid those with big holes and loose weaves that can trap small fingers, and leave beaded or sequinned fabrics for later stages.

Heads Up, Lookers and Communicators

Babies (8-20 months)

Sit with babies and cover a toy or basket with a piece of fabric so the baby can pull it off to reveal the toy. This gives great pleasure and is an 'Again, again' activity! Peep-bo! with a piece of fabric over your head is another favourite. They will soon join in with their own piece of fabric. Use different textures of fabrics for sitting on indoors and outside - try fake grass indoors or fleece on the grass, or a blanket on the patio or path. Supervise carefully to avoid tripping by unsteady toddlers.

Sitters, Standers and Explorers

Young children (16-26 months)

Make little dens indoors and outside by putting fabrics over furniture or small pieces of climbing apparatus. Make sure these are steady and firm because children at this stage may not be completely firm on their feet, and may try to pull the fabric off or steady themselves by grabbing the fabric or the structure. Drape a blanket over a clothes line or tie the corners of a big piece of fabric to fences or bushes to make a big awning or den.

Movers, Shakers and Players

Children (22-40 months)

At this stage, children begin to take control of their own creative experiences and will call on you when they need help or additional resources. Given practice, freedom and plenty of easy joining materials such as pegs, elastic and tape, individuals, pairs and groups will work on their own projects with you in attendance, ensuring safe and successful play. Big pieces of fabric can also be used to line sand, water and builders' trays for small world dramatic play.

Walkers, Talkers and Pretenders

Older children (40-60+ months)

Joining, fixing and suspending big pieces of fabric gives older children great practice in working together and problem solving. Covering a climbing frame or a bush with fabric, or suspending it from a fence or wall to make a sunshade or shelter can engage children for long periods of time, and their pleasure at success in these big projects is a real joy to see. You could try adding big sheets of plastic (dust covers are cheap and very easy to work with, but need careful supervision).

Moving on

17

Face Paints

Children have always loved make-up, and face paints give them a safe opportunity to decorate their faces hands (and bodies). Simple, home-made face paints add a new dimension to role play for children of all ages. They are easy to make, safe to play with and easy to remove if you use the recipes on these pages! Check for allergies before doing face painting.

Young babies (0-11 months)

This recipe is safe to use with babies. You can put a dab of colour on their nose, cheeks or fingers, knowing that even if they suck or lick it off, they will be safe, and it will wash out of clothes.

Recipe 1

Mix together:
1 tablespoon moisturiser
(use a perfume free variety)
2 tablespoons cornflour
1 tablespoon water
a few drops of food colouring
Apply anywhere on the skin.

Heads Up, Lookers and Communicators

Babies (8-20 months)

Offer little saucers or bowls of face paint to babies so they can explore it with their fingers and spread it on their hands and feet. Make sure they are in a suitable state of dress, and don't worry if they just explore! Single colours are easier to manage, and if mirrors are a current interest for them, you could put the activity in front of an unbreakable mirror. Join in the fun by exploring the paint yourself and painting on your own hands and face.

Sitters, Standers and Explorers

Young children (16-26 months)

Recipe 2

Mix together:
30ml baby lotion
(a non-allergenic sort)
1 squeeze of washing up liquid
1/4 teaspoon dry or ready mixed powder paint
Apply anywhere on the skin.

Children may like to use this face paint on dolls' faces and bodies, then give them a bubble bath afterwards. They will still enjoy painting their own faces (and bodies too if you let them) so you could offer this activity outside on a warm day.

Movers, Shakers and Players

Children (22-40 months)

As they become more aware of others, children at this stage may find it easier to apply the paints on their friends (if they are willing), as this is much easier than trying to paint your own face, specially in a mirror! Try adding some body painting sticks such as glitter face paint or face painting pencils. Set up a table with a mirror on a stand, so children can sit to paint their faces. Using fingers is still easier than brushes. Decorating dolls is still a popular activity.

Walkers, Talkers and Pretenders

Older children (40-60+ months)

Older children may like to use cotton buds or fine brushes to paint their own or others' faces, but stay with them to help with safe work. As role play develops, children may like to make 'tattoos', 'jewels' or superhero marks on their arms and hands as they get involved in a range of roles. Remember that role play is a really good vehicle for practicing hand-eye control and developing creative thinking. Cocoa powder is a good colouring for brown face paint.

Moving on

19

Boxes (large)

Big boxes and cartons have hundreds of uses in role play. Never refuse the offer of a big box, and ask for the packaging from big items such as TVs, washing machines and fridges. If you ask suppliers to flatten them for you they should fit in your car, or you could take the children for a walk to collect some!

Remember to check all boxes before use – look for and remove serrated edges, metal cutting edges and staples.

Young babies (0-11 months)

Big boxes make great places to share with babies. Put the box on its side or upright, climb in with a baby and perhaps a cushion, and enjoy a new look on the world. You could sing, play with a toy or take a torch inside to make it even more exciting. Some babies like lying in a shallow carton like a cot, others hate it - so check before making any assumptions and don't leave them there too long.

Heads Up, Lookers and Communicators

Babies (8-20 months)

Leave big cartons on their sides for babies to crawl or scramble into. Hide toys, cushions or other tempting objects inside, perhaps a toy that makes a noise or lights up. Some sitting babies find great comfort in sitting in an upright box as it seems to give them a sense of security. Some babies will even sit right underneath an upside-down box, so you could cut some peep-holes in the sides of some of the boxes you offer.

Sitters, Standers and Explorers

Young children (16-26 months)

At this stage, you can use big boxes for all sorts of games and activities. Cut both ends out to make tunnels, join boxes together to make longer ones, cut windows and doors so the children can see out. Add ropes to boxes so children can tug them along. Replace the boxes as they become worn, or give them a coat of emulsion paint to extend their life. Make sure there are plenty of boxes as they will be popular with all the children.

Movers, Shakers and Players

Children (22-40 months)

By this stage, children will be exploring all sorts of role play situations and will love to have big boxes and cartons to add to or customise for their play. Let them paint and decorate the cars, buses, rockets, houses and shelters they are making. Diluted emulsion paint is cheap and washes out of clothes and hair, and they can use decorating brushes to cover big areas quickly. Help them to cut doors, windows etc. as this will need a craft knife.

Walkers, Talkers and Pretenders

Older children (40-60+ months)

A pile of big empty cartons and other packaging is a really good independent activity for older children. Of course they will need you to be around to help with the difficult bits, but a collection of boxes, ropes, tyres, planks and other large scale recycled materials will provide endless hours of fun and creativity which will involve children in working together to make decisions and construct on a big scale.

Moving on

Boxes (small)

Collections of small boxes, tubes, cartons, plastic pots, lolly sticks, straws and other recycled or bargain price materials will enhance children's role play by providing inspiration for making props and other role play items. Joining materials should also be available.

Remember to check all boxes before use – look for and remove serrated edges, metal cutting edges and staples.

Young babies (0-11 months)

Choose a small selection of recycled materials and explore these with the baby. Feel the materials and handle them, passing them to each other, or just looking at their textures and shapes. Look inside the boxes, peep at each other through the tumes. Babies need plenty of this sort of experience of materials long before they can start to manipulate them by themselves and turn them into other things.

Heads Up, Lookers and Communicators

Babies (8-20 months)

During this stage, some babies will begin to explore how one object can represent another. They will use a doll's hair brush or a toothbrush to 'brush' their own hair, or use a plate as a 'steering wheel', or a soft toy as a 'baby'. Some children will only come to this stage later, and others will need to be introduced to the idea of using things to make other things. Sit with babies and explore a box of recycled materials, looking through tubes, opening and shutting boxes.

Sitters, Standers and Explorers

Young children (16-26 months)

As young children begin to understand that role play is more than hats and shoes, they will start to use objects to enhance their play. They may use stones or sticks as gifts or treasure. They may start to explore containers and other props, but these will probably still be real-life objects such as brushes, bags, blankets and beds. They may make small beds for soft toys or use a box as a garage for a small car or a cage for a small world animal.

Movers, Shakers and Players

Children (22-40 months)

As children's knowledge of the world of playing in role expands through stories, visits and other experiences, they will begin to think of roles in terms of props as well as costumes. They will want a tool kit for a mechanic, a crown for a princess, a telescope for a pirate - and a plentiful supply of all sorts of materials and easy ways of fixing them will ensure that they can make their own simple props independently or with the minimum of help from you.

Walkers, Talkers and Pretenders

Older children (40-60+ months)

If children are encouraged to experiment and make their own props for role play the play will become more rich and complex. Children will often work for long periods constructing and perfecting their own props using recycled materials, and they will often bring things from home to use too. Try to use your own imagination as you collect new materials for children to use. Some of these may be free, others may be cheap purchases such as plastic cups, straws, envelopes, paper plates, lolly sticks, plant ties etc.

Moving on

Sticks and Canes

Garden sticks, canes and twigs are other key resources for role play with young children. Of course, you will have to help them to build their constructions, certainly at first, but older children will soon learn simple fixings for structures of all sorts and scales, working together to solve problems and adapt their work.

Young babies (0-11 months)

Use canes to make a simple wigwam and sit inside with the baby, to share a book, sing some songs or just watch the world go by. Babies also enjoy watching older children work and play, and the older children might like to get involved in making shelters and dens for babies.

Heads Up, Lookers and Communicators

Babies (8-20 months)

Use sticks and twigs to make little houses, tents, wigwams and shelters. Cover these with thin fabric and put a cushion or rug inside. Babies will love to lie, sit or crawl into these little places, where they can rest, chat, sing or play with favourite toys, with or without an adult close by. Make sure the canes and sticks are firmly fixed together and secured to the ground by sticking them in earth or grass, or weighting them down with bricks, as babies tend to grab and pull everything.

Sitters, Standers and Explorers

Young children (16-26 months)

As children become more mobile, you can use twigs, sticks and canes to make tunnels and caves, covering these with fabrics or plastic sheets. Waterproof structures are good fun outside in the rain, and a snack or a little picnic in a tent indoors is a lovely change from the normal snack period. Wigwams covered with plastic sheeting can be decorated or even have doors or windows cut in. These can be holes or flaps with stick-on Velcro fasteners.

Movers, Shakers and Players

Children (22-40 months)

Use sticks and canes to build more permanent structures, including growing plants such as beans, nasturtiums and other climbers. You can tie canes at the top with string or elastic to make a traditional wigwam shape, or lean them at an angle against a wall or the side of a shed, securing the bottoms of the canes in the ground. Once the plants begin to grow, they will secure the canes in place and you will just need to trim the growth so children can get inside.

Walkers, Talkers and Pretenders

Older children (40-60+ months)

Living Willow is a superb way of making permanent structures. Find a supplier near you by searching the internet. Help children to plant these sticks to make living wigwams, tunnels, seats or shelters that will keep growing, only needing annual pruning. The children will love playing inside these structures and turning them into houses and other role play situations. Older children will also enjoy making smaller structures from green garden sticks or bamboo canes and covering them with plastic or fabric for use with small world animals, play people or superhero figures.

Moving on

Underneath

The spaces underneath things are very important to children of all ages. Hiding under or behind things, or being covered up are great fun, providing secret spaces where children can become invisible - sharing secrets, playing with friends or getting some quiet time. Make some of these spaces available in your setting for role play.

Young babies (0-11 months)

Find some 'underneath' spaces to share with babies - even sitting under a table, perhaps with a piece of thin fabric hanging over the edge, will be a new experience for babies. As you sit there, talk about what you can see happening outside, the other children, adults and activities. Try sitting underneath a low canopy of fabric outside, where you can see and hear the sky, the birds, children playing etc. Take a soft toy, a book or a CD player with soothing music.

Heads Up, Lookers and Communicators

Babies (8-20 months)

Make secret places where crawling, shuffling and toddling babies can choose to be. Under tables, in corners, behind furniture are all good places. You could even erect a small pop-up tent indoors or a beach shelter outside. Leave baskets of books, small toys, or treasure baskets inside where the babies can explore them in privacy and quiet. Join the babies in these quiet places, just sitting with them and enjoying being together, or talking quietly about what they are doing.

Sitters, Standers and Explorers

Young children (16-26 months)

Large cardboard boxes, plastic cubes and tunnels can all be used as places for role playing, not just for gross motor activities. Try bringing a big plastic cube or tunnel from your outdoor play equipment indoors and putting cushions or blankets inside, with a picnic basket or a box of small world toys. These solid structures are quite different when you use them indoors and for a different purpose. Even an upturned washing basket or laundry basket will be fun for a day's play.

Movers, Shakers and Players

Children (22-40 months)

On a wet day, try covering an outdoor table with a plastic sheet or putting up a pop-up tent just outside the door, with a tunnel leading to it. Children can crawl through the tunnel and enjoy the rain while staying dry! Or offer lots of umbrellas of different sizes to shelter under from rain or sun. Children love having simple ready-made structures, such as clothes airers or small pieces of lightweight climbing apparatus that they can cover themselves with a sheet to make a den.

Walkers, Talkers and Pretenders

Older children (40-60+ months)

Older children will enjoy experimenting with clips, pegs or strings to make covers, roofs and canopies of their own. Help them to find out how they could cover the bottom of the climbing frame for a house, the top of the climbing frame for a castle or lighthouse, a table or A-frame for a den. Or they could make canopies for garages and car washes, gazebos for garden centres or barbecues, marquees for weddings or sunshades for picnics or seaside settings.

Moving on

Screens

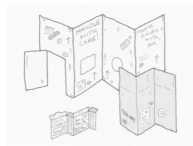

Screens are extremely versatile resources for role play. Ideally they should be lightweight and stable so older children can move them about themselves in safety. Making your own screens is easy if you use the sides of big packing cartons or large rolls of corrugated card available from educational suppliers.

Young babies (0-11 months)

Exploring the openings and windows in screens is a fascinating activity for babies. Hold them so they can see through the windows and doors in home corner screens, both from the inside and the outside, talking about what you can see and hear. Screens can be used to make quiet areas for rest times, and provide you with surfaces for displays, photos and other favourite images for each baby.

Heads Up, Lookers and Communicators

Babies (8-20 months)

Screens can be used to encourage babies to move and reach for objects and to move from space to space. Cut big boxes down the joins, so they become screens (see illustration) then cut shapes low down in the screens so babies can crawl or creep through them. Make sure the screen is securely fixed to avoid accidental squashing! Low screens made from plywood or hardboard, with wooden feet to steady them are excellent places for mirrors or for toddlers to lean on.

Sitters, Standers and Explorers

Young children (16-26 months)

Use screens to make quick and flexible role play areas indoors or outside. They can divide a space to protect younger children from rushing bikes and wheeled toys, or provide an instant shop, puppet theatre, castle or quiet place to sit with a basket of small world toys. Wooden and carton screens can be painted with blackboard paint for drawing, writing or sign making with chalks, and paint to turn them into real places.

Movers, Shakers and Players

Children (22-40 months)

Carton screens are very versatile, as they fold easily for storage and are light to carry and move around. Screens can also be used for more unusual and short term role play areas such as a caravan, a pirate ship, a palace, vet, café or fast food outlet. You could also expand the role play by having an area inside linked to another outside - a house inside with a post office outside, a pizza place outside delivering pizzas to a house inside.

Walkers, Talkers and Pretenders

Older children (40-60+ months)

By the time children get to this stage they will enjoy helping to customise screens by painting them with emulsion paint and adding window boxes, door numbers and other door furniture, signs and notices. Puppet show screens can be quickly made and given smart stripes or patterns. House screens can have flowers, brick patterns or door and window frames. Shops can have signs and adverts in their (plastic sheeting) windows or on their doors.

Moving on

Vehicles

Some vehicles lend themselves immediately to role play situations, others can be quickly and easily customised if you think creatively about materials and resources. Make sure you have lengths of rope, flexible sticks and canes, plastic sheeting and waterproof markers handy, and encourage children to be creative too.

Young babies (0-11 months)

Your equipment will probably include small trucks and trolleys that you can use with even small babies, propping them securely with cushions or blankets, so they can go for tiny rides, pulled along by you. If you haven't got a trolley, a strong cardboard or wooden box can be used instead. Babies love being on the move, and will enjoy these little rides with you. They will also love to sit with you and watch older children playing with wheeled toys.

Heads Up, Lookers and Communicators

Babies (8-20 months)

As babies become more independent, baby walkers, trucks, wheelbarrows and ride-on toys will be very popular. They will be the focus for pushing, loading, unloading and moving favourite items around. Make sure you have plenty of simple, light vehicles for pushing, pulling and scooting along. Small lightweight pushchairs, lawn mowers and vacuum cleaners will also be popular as children become interested in playing out the things they see adults do.

Sitters, Standers and Explorers

Young children (16-26 months)

Children at this age love putting things in and taking them out, and small world vehicles such as fire engines, Noah's Arks, aeroplanes, tractors and trains give plenty of opportunities for early role play about their experiences of the real world. Ride-on toys may also be popular, and play with these can be enhanced by offering hats, bags, badges or things to carry in trailers or baskets. Job specific vehicles can help children to extend their play beyond just riding.

Movers, Shakers and Players

Children (22-40 months)

This is the age of riding, scooting, pushing, pulling, carrying and tipping. Children of this age love vehicles of all sorts, and will often have a favourite which they ride exclusively. Provide bikes and trikes with and without pedals, small cars and steering wheels, three wheeled scooters, baby walkers, barrows, push-chairs and any others you can find. Make sure there are vehicles to appeal to all children whatever their interests, gender or physical maturity.

Walkers, Talkers and Pretenders

Older children (40-60+ months)

Encourage the children to personalise and decorate vehicles to meet their current interests by adding stickers, notices, flags, pennants and tassels. Fix baskets and small trailers to the backs and fronts of bikes and trikes. Help them to make hats, headbands and badges to wear, and use backpacks, bags, baby slings and other containers to carry essential items - tools for a mechanic, letters for a postman, pizzas, babies. Make flags easily from plastic carrier bags cut into triangles and squares.

Moving on

Bags, Cases and Boxes

Containers are essential items for successful role play, so collect as many different sorts as you can beg, borrow or buy cheaply, and don't forget to ask parents and colleagues for unwanted ones. Include small suitcases and carry-on bags with wheels, bags, backpacks, baskets, boxes, gift bags and boxes, tool boxes, pet boxes.

Young babies (0-11 months)

Paper bags to scrunch and squash, fabric drawstring bags with small toys or sound makers inside, boxes that rattle, textured bags to feel and handle. These simple containers are some of the first puzzles that babies encounter, making them look, listen, think and explore. Changing bags and handbags hold a fascination for babies and small children, and little baskets and bags are often favourite toys, even when they are empty.

Heads Up, Lookers and Communicators

Babies (8-20 months)

The in and out of containers will fascinate babies - posting boxes, containers with lids, pop up toys and toys that open when you press buttons or twist knobs. Taking things out of bags and baskets will fascinate many babies for long periods of time, so baskets of socks or treasure baskets of everyday objects will help babies to make relationships between the things in their lives. Sit with them as they take things out and put them in, exploring and handling them as they play.

Sitters, Standers and Explorers

Young children (16-26 months)

One of the best ways to introduce a new item of clothing for role play, a new puppet or soft toy, or a book, is to put it in a bag, box or other container and use this at group time, or leave it for children to find themselves. Make some role play bags that can be used over time, perhaps some decorating equipment for painting with water, some builders' hard hats, plastic money and a simple till for an impromptu shop, cooking utensils for make-believe cooking.

Movers, Shakers and Players

Children (22-40 months)

Containers can be creative ways of introducing new themes for role play, maybe linked to your current curriculum theme - a small suitcase full of holiday clothes, a bag for a Bear Hunt, crowns and jewels in a royal velvet bag, a lost soft toy with a label round his neck, a surprise gift in a shiny box, some minibeasts. Children also love to have bags and baskets to carry their favourite toys in as they move around the setting, giving them a sense of security.

Walkers, Talkers and Pretenders

Older children (40-60+ months)

Backpacks and wheeled suitcases made for children are favourites at this stage. Many children will have used these on holiday, and they will inspire a lot of play about travelling. Offer plenty of suitable items and holiday clothing and hats to pack, and encourage children to make labels and tickets for their holidays. You could turn your home corner into a hotel or beach resort and offer some bare-foot sand and water experiences outside in builders' trays or bowls.

Moving on

Jewels, Badges, Glasses and Decorations

These are the extras that enhance any outfit and really make the character someone to contend with! Beads, brooches, badges, sunglasses, spectacle frames, bracelets and bangles, ribbons, hair slides and scrunchies, old watches, purses and evening bags are just some of the things you can find or ask for from families and friends.

Young babies (0-11 months)

Just looking at a brooch or string of beads with you is a good starting point for young babies. Sit with them and explore something safe - a plastic bangle, some big beads or a brooch with the safety clasp closed. Check all resources for sharp edges, pins, or loose parts which may be risky. Stick to objects that can be easily washed and are tooth and dribble proof!

Heads Up, Lookers and Communicators

Babies (8-20 months)

Add <u>safe</u> jewellery to treasure baskets and other collections for exploration. You could include plastic and metal bangles, chunky wrist and neck chains, brooches and badges with pins and loose parts removed, glasses frames (with and without cases), purses with clips and zips. Make sure the items can't be swallowed and are washable. Or you could play a glasses game with the sitting babies, trying on glasses together from a collection in a basket.

Sitters, Standers and Explorers

Young children (16-26 months)

Adult and children's glasses make great role play accessories and often inspire new play or characters. Add some to a basket of hats and gloves for a different sort of role play activity. Opticians will sometimes donate samples of children's glasses frames, or you could ask families and colleagues to donate unused pairs of adult and children's frames. You can often buy cheap children's sunglasses from bargain shops or seaside gift shops, particularly at the end of the season.

Movers, Shakers and Players

Children (22-40 months)

Bead threading will result in necklaces that will often be worn for whole days, and given as special gifts to adults and friends, so try to offer some imaginative things to thread - tube pasta dyed with food colouring (put dry pasta in a zip-lock bag with a few drops of colouring), polystyrene, leaves, paper clips, plastic straws cut into lengths. Or help them make their own badges and jewels from playdough and bake them hard. Hand and full length mirrors are essential to this activity.

Walkers, Talkers and Pretenders

Older children (40-60+ months)

By this stage, children will be interested in making all the accompaniments to role play - superhero armbands and wrist-bands, headbands, crowns, badges, bracelets, wedding jewels, pirate eye-patches and ear-rings, magic wands, treasure boxes and many other small and specific additions to particular characters and scenarios. Make sure there are plenty of resources to inspire them - foil, beads, sequins, card, fabric, ribbon, cord and recycled materials.

Moving on

35

Projectors and Screens

Overhead projectors and interactive whiteboards are far more common in settings now, so if you have one or can borrow one, don't forget to use it to inspire role play too. If you haven't got a projector try ask in a local school, conference centre or hotel, they may have an old one you can have, as they move to newer technology.

Young babies (0-11 months)

Use an OHP (overhead projector) or IWB (interactive whiteboard) to show babies pictures of people and objects. You can just put objects on an OHP table and project their shadows on a screen. If you have an IWB, you can collect photos of babies' families, favourite toys, animals or other significant things. You could also add some photos of the babies themselves, just as they are. Don't spend too long on this, monitor their attention and interest.

Heads Up, Lookers and Communicators

Babies (8-20 months)

Take digital photos of the babies wearing different items of clothing - hats, glasses, cloaks, big shoes, so they can look at themselves on the screen. You can leave a picture on an OHP screen so the babies can crawl or toddle over and touch the image of themselves. Add some photos of familiar adults wearing special clothes, soft toys, story character puppets, TV characters and people who help us, such as doctors, firemen, police etc.

Sitters, Standers and Explorers

Young children (16-26 months)

Use an interactive white board to project stories and film clips which can inspire new role play and help children understand sequencing and new characters. Then you can provide a simple role play bag of props for the children to use as they retell the story. You could also video or photograph role play in action in your setting and show the results to children so they can see themselves playing and creating, or use Powerpoint to make presentations of photos.

Movers, Shakers and Players

Children (22-40 months)

Children should now be able to use an OHP machine independently to project pictures and objects. They will also be able to relate to real life figures, vehicles and situations which may affect and contribute to their role play. You could project scenes and vehicles onto an IWB and let children add their own characters and additional scenery, tools or clothing. You could also project pictures of clothing, equipment or tools so children can talk about who uses them.

Walkers, Talkers and Pretenders

Older children (40-60+ months)

Use a projector to project a backdrop for play, so children can play in role in front of the screen. Or project a drawing or photo on a wall and paint a big backdrop using the scene as a guide. You could then replicate your local fish and chip shop, baker, garden centre or fire station. If you paint it on a sheet with thin paint, you can use it, then roll it up for next time you need that role play focus. Or you could do this outside, projecting the scene on a wall and drawing round it to make a mural.

Moving on

Outside

Your outdoor area, however small, can offer many opportunities for role play, both with whole bodies and the small worlds of soft toys, puppets, play people model animals and small vehicles. Invest in some builders' trays for small world work, and use your imagination in making areas where children can play creatively. You don't need fixed equipment or expensive resources.

Young babies (0-11 months)

Sit on a blanket or cushion outside with a baby, playing with simple props and items of dressing up clothing such as hats, glasses and shoes. Make a little shelter to sit in, and play a little game or sing a song. Watch the other children playing with role play materials, join in their games in tents and shelters, talk with babies about what the older children are doing.

Heads Up, Lookers and Communicators

Babies (8-20 months)

As soon as babies are on the move, they should be able to access the outdoor area independently. Think about how this can be made easy for them. Let them take soft toys, dolls and other toys outside with them, and offer boxes, small trucks, cots and little pushchairs for them to play with. Tea sets and other home corner play can be offered in shallow baskets on a blanket, and you can easily construct a sun canopy with a piece of light fabric.

Sitters, Standers and Explorers

Young children (16-26 months)

Prop boxes of role play items can be introduced at this stage. Show the children where they are kept and they will be able to help themselves. Open boxes or baskets are easier for this age, and you can use simple props for well known people such as the postman, fireman, or princess. Add props for characters in stories - these could be simple headbands or animal ears. Provide small world sets in builders' trays and puppets or soft toys out of doors.

Movers, Shakers and Players

Children (22-40 months)

This is the age when many children spend all day being someone else, so they will play in role outside as well as indoors. Make sure you have outdoor equipment for all interests by providing domestic play as well as vehicles, small world versions as well as whole body play, and expand your collection of prop boxes and bags by adding backpacks to wear while riding, tools for mending the vehicles, and a home setting in some sort of shelter.

Walkers, Talkers and Pretenders

Older children (40-60+ months)

Once they have the practice, and if you give them the permission, older children will build their own structures out of doors to support their imaginative play. Provide them with ropes, buckets, pulleys, flags, pop-up tents, canes, sticks, fabric and pegs, sheets of plastic, bags and containers. Add a trolley or table with a box of recycled materials and equipment for making their own props, masks and hats and children will spend long periods constructing their own worlds. Play will become complex, involving different groups as they add new elements to stories.

Moving on

Existing and planned titles in the Baby and Beyond series include:

* Messy Play (ready now)
* The Sensory World (ready now)
* Sound and Music (ready now)
* The Natural World (ready now)
* Construction (ready now)
* Mark Making (ready now)
* Puppets, Soft Toys & Dolls (ready now)

* Bikes, Prams & Pushchairs (ready)
* Finger Play and Rhymes (ready)
* Role Play (ready now)
* Cooking (2007)
* Small World Play (2007)
* Stories, Songs, Rhymes (2008)
* Counting (2008)